Finding Patterns

Plant Patterns

by Nathan Olson

Mankato, Minnesota

A+ Books are published by Capstone Press,
1710 Roe Crest Drive, North Mankato, Minnesota 56003.
www.capstonepub.com

Books published by Capstone Press are manufactured with paper
containing at least 10 percent post-consumer waste.

Library of Congress Cataloging-in-Publication Data
Olson, Nathan.
    Plant patterns / by Nathan Olson.
    p. cm.—(A+ books. Finding patterns)
    Summary: "Simple text and color photographs introduce different kinds of plant
patterns"—Provided by publisher.
    Includes bibliographical references and index.
    ISBN-13: 978-0-7368-6727-6 (hardcover)   ISBN-10: 0-7368-6727-9 (hardcover)
    ISBN-13: 978-0-7368-7845-6 (softcover pbk.)   ISBN-10: 0-7368-7845-9 (softcover pbk.)
    1. Pattern perception—Juvenile literature. 2. Plants—Miscellanea—Juvenile literature. I. Title. II. Series.
BF294.O56 2007
516'.15—dc22   2006018188

Credits

Jenny Marks, editor; Renée Doyle, designer; Charlene Deyle, photo researcher;
    Scott Thoms, photo editor

Photo Credits

Corbis/Bob Krist, 7; Corbis/Darrell Gulin, 10; Corbis/Jon Hicks, 6; Corbis/Jose Fuste Raga, 11;
Corbis/Neil Miller; Papilio, 25; Corbis/Richard Hamilton Smith, 22; Corbis/William Manning, 13
(inset); Getty Images Inc./Stone/Chad Ehlers, 16–17; James P. Rowan, 20, 26–27; Richard Cummins,
24; Robert McCaw, 12–13, 14, 23; Shutterstock/Bonnie J. Anderson, 21; Shutterstock/Joshua Haviv,
cover (bouquet); Shutterstock/Lexy Sinnott, 4–5; Shutterstock/Nancy Tunison, cover (hosta leaves),
1; Shutterstock/Neil Webster, 18–19; Shutterstock/Peter Igel, 8–9; Shutterstock/Sarah Spencer, 29;
Shutterstock/Tischenko Irina, 15

Note to Parents, Teachers, and Librarians

Finding Patterns uses color photographs and a nonfiction format to introduce readers to seeing
patterns in the real world. *Plant Patterns* is designed to be read aloud to a pre-reader, or to be read
independently by an early reader. Images and activities encourage mathematical thinking in early
readers and listeners. The book encourages further learning by including the following sections: Table
of Contents, Plant Pattern Facts, Glossary, Read More, Internet Sites, and Index. Early readers may
need assistance using these features.

Printed in the United States of America in North Mankato, Minnesota.
092012   006924

Table of Contents

What Is a Pattern?

A pattern is made by a repeated shape or color. Let's look for patterns in the world of plants.

Each of these trees looks
exactly like the others.
Trees trimmed to look
the same make a pattern.

Plants trimmed into green, leafy animal shapes look fun, but they do not form a pattern.

Color Patterns

Bleeding heart flowers
bloom in a color pattern.
Each pink flower repeats
the same white stripe.

Rows of tulips, all the same shade, make a single-color pattern. Rows repeat the same colorful stripes.

Gardeners make patterns by the way they plant different colored flowers.

Row and Ring Patterns

Rows of prickly spines on a cactus make a repeating pattern. Look closer. Do you see a star pattern?

Farmers plant rows of corn. The tops grow into a pattern of tassel stripes.

Look closely and you'll see that each ear of corn has its own repeating rows of yellow kernels.

Bamboo can grow as tall as a tree, but it is really a grass. A pattern of rings circles each green stalk.

Tree trunks grow their own patterns. Each year, the tree adds a new ring.

Wildly Wonderful Patterns

Ferns uncurl in a spiral pattern called a fiddlehead.

Before they scatter,
dandelion seeds burst into
a pattern of tiny stars.

A sunflower's yellow petals grow in a pattern around the blossom's middle.

Seeds in the center of a sunflower swirl in a pattern of green and gold.

You wouldn't want
to sit on a heliconia's
pattern! Its leaves repeat
a pointy, red shape.

When a Venus flytrap snaps shut, a pattern of spiky hairs helps trap its food inside.

Plants sprout many patterns
of stripes, spots, colors,
and shapes.

Plant Pattern Facts

Tulip farms grow tulips in long rows, just like corn, soybeans, and other crops. The different colored flowers make colorful striped patterns in springtime.

Long ago, kings and queens decorated the grounds around their palaces with pretty patterns of blooming flowers and plants. Today, many public gardens grow flowers in patterns for visitors to enjoy.

Sometimes a tree is actually older than the number of rings you can count. Damage caused by a drought can cause a tree to skip adding a ring for the year.

Some people think the prickly spines on a cactus are a kind of leaf. But leaves are living parts of a plant. Even though a cactus spine grows, the only living part is its base.

A fiddlehead fern gets its name from the plant's spiral growing pattern. The young fern sprout looks similar to the scroll at the top, or head, of a fiddle.

Sunflower seeds grow in spirals that alternate right and left. Most sunflowers have 34 spirals in one direction and 55 in the other. Some very large sunflowers may have 89 spirals in one direction and 144 in the other.

Glossary

bamboo (bam-BOO)—a tropical grass with a hard, hollow stem

fern (FURN)—a plant with feathery leaves and no flowers

fiddlehead (FID-uhl-hed)—the top part of a young fern that unrolls as the fern grows

heliconia (heel-uh-KOHN-ee-uh)—a plant with bright, pointy leaves that grow opposite of one another

kernel (KUR-nul)—a grain or seed of corn

shade (SHAYD)—the lightness or darkness of a color

spine (SPINE)—a hard, sharp, pointed growth such as a thorn or cactus needle

stalk (STAWK)—the long main part or stem of a plant

tassel (TASS-uhl)—the top part of a corn stalk

Venus flytrap (VEE-nuhss FLYE-trap)—a plant that catches insects by snapping its leaves closed; it then eats its prey.

Read More

Boothroyd, Jennifer. *Patterns.* First Step Nonfiction. Minneapolis: LernerClassroom, 2007.

Jacobs, Daniel. *Patterns.* Yellow Umbrella Books for Early Readers. Bloomington, Minn.: Yellow Umbrella, 2006.

Roy, Jennifer Rozines, and Gregory Roy. *Patterns in Nature.* Math All Around. New York: Marshall Cavendish Benchmark, 2006.

Internet Sites

FactHound offers a safe, fun way to find Internet sites related to this book. All of the sites on FactHound have been researched by our staff.

Here's how:

1. Go to *www.facthound.com*
2. Select your grade level.
3. Type in this book ID **0736867279** for age-appropriate sites. You may also browse subjects by clicking on the letters, or by clicking on pictures and words
4. Click on the **Fetch It** button.

FactHound will fetch the best sites for you!

Index